Text by Geronimo Stilton
Based on the original idea by Elisabetta Dami
Illustrations by Piemme Archives

www.geronimostilton.com

© Atlantyca S.p.A. – via Leopardi 8, 20123 Milano, Italia – foreignrights@atlantyca.it

© 2015 for this Work in English language, Scholastic Education International (Singapore) Private Limited. A division of Scholastic Inc.
SCHOLASTIC and associated logos are trademarks and/or registered trademarks of Scholastic Inc.

Visit our website: www.scholastic.com.sg

First edition 2015

ISBN 978-981-4629-63-8

Stilton is the name of a famous English cheese. It is a registered trademark of the Stilton Cheese Makers' Association. For more information go to www.stiltoncheese.com

Welcome to the
Geronimo Stilton
ACADEMY

Well-loved for its humor, fascinating visuals and fun characters, the best-selling *Geronimo Stilton* series is enjoyed by children in many countries.

Research shows that learners learn better when they are engaged and motivated. The **Geronimo Stilton Academy: Comprehension Pawbook** series builds on children's interest in Geronimo Stilton. It makes learning more accessible, and increases learners' motivation to read and develop their reading comprehension skills.

The series comprises three levels:

Level 1	Level 2	Level 3
• predicting • inferring • sequencing • comparing and contrasting • recalling details and main ideas	All skills covered in Level 1 and • drawing conclusions • summarizing	All skills covered in Levels 1 and 2 and • giving reasons • stating opinions and point of view

Geronimo Stilton titles featured in this Pawbook:

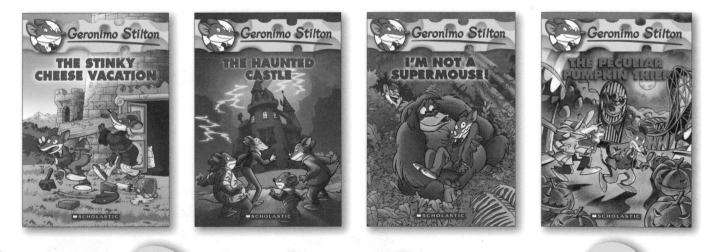

© 2015 Scholastic Education International (S) Pte Ltd ISBN 978-981-4629-63-8

Motivating learners
Excerpts from *Geronimo Stilton* titles interest and encourage learners to read the rest of the story.

Developing comprehension skills
The 3-step format in each unit develops learners' comprehension skills and provides opportunities for independent learning.

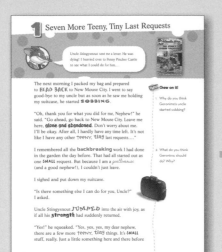

1 **Whilst-reading questions** stimulate learners to interact with the text.

2 **Comprehension questions** cover literal, inferential and higher-order reading skills for thorough understanding of the text.

3 **Graphic activities** develop learners' ability to translate what they have read and their visual text comprehension.

Extending vocabulary and understanding
Each double-page spread consists of a fun activity related to the preceding units to extend learning.

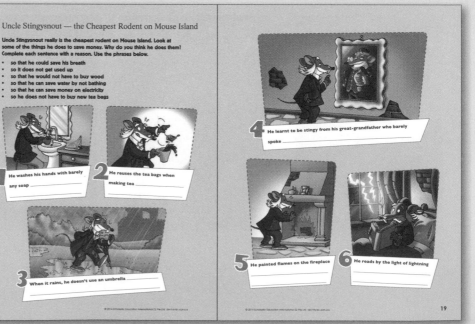

© 2015 Scholastic Education International (S) Pte Ltd   ISBN 978-981-4629-63-8

Contents

© 2015 Scholastic Education International (S) Pte Ltd ISBN 978-981-4629-63-8

Uncle Stingysnout sent me a letter. He was dying! I hurried over to Penny Pincher Castle to see what I could do for him....

The next morning I packed my bag and prepared to **HEAD BACK** to New Mouse City. I went to say good-bye to my uncle but as soon as he saw me holding my suitcase, he started **SOBBING**.

"Oh, thank you for what you did for me, Nephew!" he said. "Go ahead, go back to New Mouse City. Leave me here, *alone and abandoned*. Don't worry about me. I'll be okay. After all, I hardly have any time left. It's not like I have any other TEENY, tiny last requests...."

I remembered all the **backbreaking** work I had done in the garden the day before. That had all started out as one **SMALL** request. But because I am a *gentlemouse* (and a good nephew!), I couldn't just leave.

I sighed and put down my suitcase.

"Is there something else I can do for you, Uncle?" I asked.

Uncle Stingysnout **JUMPED** into the air with joy, as if all his **strength** had suddenly returned.

"Yes!" he squeaked. "Yes, yes, yes, my dear nephew, there are a few more TEENY, tiny things. It's **SMALL** stuff, really. Just a little something here and there before

Chew on it!

1. Why do you think Geronimo's uncle started sobbing?

2. What do you think Geronimo should do? Why?

Excerpt from *The Stinky Cheese Vacation*
(Originally published in Italy by Edizioni Piemme *Ma che vacanza...a Rocca Taccagna!*)

I go to my **cold**, **DARK**, and **LONELY** grave!"

"That sounds okay," I agreed.

"Actually, it's *seven* little things!" he added **QUICKLY**.

"Seven!" I exclaimed in shock. "Yesterday you told me you had just **ONE** last request."

He **kneeled** down in front of me.

"Oh, please, please, please, with **cheese** on top?" he begged dramatically. "I don't know what I would do without a **GENEROUS**, **KINDHEARTED** nephew like you!"

"All right, I'll do it," I agreed with a sigh. How could I say **no**?

"Great!" Uncle Stingysnout announced with **satisfaction**. "Here's what I want you to do...."

3. Why was Geronimo shocked?

1. Plant a *flowery* garden around my tomb. (You've already done this one: Good job!)

2. Polish my coffin.

3. FIX my car for the funeral.

4. Find my **WILL**.

5. Sew my funeral **SUIT**.

6. Cook **DINNER** for the funeral.

7. Get the **castle** ready for the funeral.

Excerpt from *The Stinky Cheese Vacation*
(Originally published in Italy by Edizioni Piemme *Ma che vacanza...a Rocca Taccagna!*)

 **Circle the correct answers.**

1. Why did Geronimo's uncle tell him to "leave me here, **alone and abandoned**..."?

    (a)   He was happy to be left alone.

    (b)   He wanted Geronimo to go home quickly.

    (c)   He was trying to make Geronimo feel better.

    (d)   He was trying to make Geronimo feel bad about leaving.

2. Geronimo said that the work he did in the garden was "**backbreaking**". What does that tell you about the task?

    (a)   The task was easy.

    (b)   The task broke his back.

    (c)   The task was a lot of hard work.

    (d)   He had to do the task while lying on his back.

3. Why did Geronimo's uncle kneel in front of him?

    (a)   He was trying to look pitiful.

    (b)   He liked being on his knees.

    (c)   He wanted to talk to Geronimo face to face.

    (d)   He was upset that Geronimo did not want to help him and fell to his knees.

4. Geronimo's uncle had already prepared a list of things he wanted Geronimo to do. What does this tell you?

    (a)   He was trying to be funny.

    (b)   He knew Geronimo would agree to help him.

    (c)   He was satisfied with Geronimo's help.

    (d)   He would have done these things himself if Geronimo did not agree to help him.

5. How did Uncle Stingysnout get Geronimo to help even though he wanted to go home?

    (a)   He told Geronimo that there were only seven tasks.

    (b)   He said nice things about Geronimo.

    (c)   He prepared a list so Geronimo would know what to do.

    (d)   He jumped into the air for joy.

 Excerpt from *The Stinky Cheese Vacation*
(Originally published in Italy by Edizioni Piemme *Ma che vacanza...a Rocca Taccagna!*)   © 2015 Scholastic Education International (S) Pte Ltd ISBN 978-981-4629-63-8

Match each of the tasks to the correct picture. Write the correct number.

1. Plant a flowery garden around my tomb.
2. Polish and repair my coffin.
3. Fix my car for the funeral.
4. Find my will.
5. Sew my funeral suit.
6. Cook dinner for the funeral.
7. Get the castle ready for the funeral.

© 2015 Scholastic Education International (S) Pte Ltd ISBN 978-981-4629-63-8

Excerpt from *The Stinky Cheese Vacation*
(Originally published in Italy by Edizioni Piemme *Ma che vacanza…a Rocca Taccagna!*)

Today's task is to find Uncle Stingysnout's will. It should be easy! Shouldn't it?

The next morning I woke up feeling tired but **happy**: Today's task would be an **EASY** one! All I had to do was find Uncle Stingysnout's **will**.

My uncle was waiting for me in the library, where he greeted me with a **suspicious**-looking smile.

"Good morning, dear nephew," he said. "Today you have to find my will. I think it's hidden somewhere in this library, in one of these **seven thousand** books!"

I almost *fainted* when I looked **UP** at the ROWS AND ROWS of books. They never seemed to end! But how could I say **no**? So I rolled up my sleeves and began to sift through the books ONE BY ONE.

"**Erhem**." Uncle Stingysnout cleared his throat. "Since you've already started, could you also organize these books **alphabetically**? And dust them off, ONE BY ONE? You know, no one has cleaned in here for about

Chew on it!

1. What is a suspicious-looking smile?

Excerpt from *The Stinky Cheese Vacation*
(Originally published in Italy by Edizioni Piemme *Ma che vacanza...a Rocca Taccagna!*)

twenty years. I can't hire a cleaner because **IT COSTS TOO MUCH**!"

How could I say **NO**? I got to work, but in order to get to the books on the TOP shelves, I needed a ladder. I found the TALLEST one in the castle. But as I was climbing, a rung broke and I **fell** **1**. I *landed* on a wooden desk **2**, then I tumbled to the floor, massaging my head where a great big BUMP had formed **3**. Suddenly, I noticed something strange **4**. Falling onto the desk had activated a **HIDDEN** mechanism that was linked to a *SECRET* drawer. The drawer had opened, and inside was a rolled-up SCROLL! I grabbed the scroll and ran to find Uncle Stingysnout **5**.

"Uncle, I think I found your will!" I **squeaked**.

Uncle Stingysnout grabbed the scroll and *stuffed* it in his pocket.

"No, no," he said quickly. "It's not my will, UNFORTUNATELY."

2. What would your room look like if you didn't clean it for 2 weeks?

3. Do you think the will is in the library? Why?

© 2015 Scholastic Education International (S) Pte Ltd ISBN 978-981-4629-63-8

(Originally published in Italy by Edizioni Piemme Ma che vacanza...a Rocca Taccagna!)

Excerpt from *The Stinky Cheese Vacation*

Circle the correct answers.

1. Who was in the library first?

   (a) Geronimo

   (b) Uncle Stingysnout

   (c) The cleaner

   (d) Geronimo and Uncle Stingysnout got there at the same time.

2. Why hasn't the library been cleaned for so long?

   (a) Uncle Stingysnout thinks it is too expensive.

   (b) Uncle Stingysnout does not have the money to pay a cleaner.

   (c) There are too many books.

   (d) It is dangerous to clean the books on the top shelves.

3. Why couldn't Geronimo just say "**NO**" to Uncle Stingysnout?

   (a) Uncle Stingysnout was his favorite uncle.

   (b) Uncle Stingysnout lied and tricked him.

   (c) Geronimo was kindhearted and his dying uncle needed his help.

   (d) Geronimo secretly liked working hard and saving money for his uncle.

4. What do you think Uncle Stingysnout really wanted Geronimo to do?

   (a) Find his will

   (b) Read all the books in his library

   (c) Dust the books and arrange them alphabetically

   (d) Find the rolled-up scroll

5. Why organize the books alphabetically?

   (a) It will make the books look neater.

   (b) It will make looking for a book easy.

   (c) Uncle Stingysnout wanted to see if Geronimo knew the alphabet.

   (d) It would be easy and fast to do.

 Excerpt from *The Stinky Cheese Vacation*
(Originally published in Italy by Edizioni Piemme *Ma che vacanza...a Rocca Taccagna!*) © 2015 Scholastic Education International (S) Pte Ltd ISBN 978-981-4629-63-8

What happened to Geronimo after the ladder broke?
Number the pictures 1, 2, 3, 4 and 5 to show what happened.

Excerpt from *The Stinky Cheese Vacation*
(Originally published in Italy by Edizioni Piemme *Ma che vacanza…a Rocca Taccagna!*)

3 Get The Castle Ready … And That's It!

> I had been working very hard to complete Uncle Stingysnout's list. One thing was to get the castle ready for his funeral. I wonder what that means…

The next morning when I **WOKE UP** I was still leaning against the freezer.

"Good **morning**, Nephew!" Uncle Stingysnout squeaked happily. "Today, you will fulfill my very **LAST** wish: get Penny Pincher Castle ready for the **FUNERAL**! But it might take more than a **DAY** to do it. . . ."

I was *worried*. "What exactly do you mean by '**GET THE CASTLE READY**'?" I asked.

"Erhem, well . . ." he said, **clearing** his throat and pulling out a very **LOOOONG** list. "My dearest nephew, this is what I mean by '**GET THE CASTLE READY**': paint the walls and ceilings, **WAX** the floors, **REDO** the electrical system, **repair** the plumbing, clean the sewers, **RESTORE** the roof, **install** heating and air-conditioning, and **transform** the pond into a heated swimming pool! I wish I could hire a contractor to do it, but as you know, dear nephew, **IT COSTS TOO MUCH!**"

I couldn't take it anymore! I took one look at the list and I **FAINTED**.

Chew on it!

1. Why do you think it might take more than a day to get the castle ready?

2. Do you think the list of things is fair?

Excerpt from *The Stinky Cheese Vacation*
(Originally published in Italy by Edizioni Piemme *Ma che vacanza…a Rocca Taccagna!*)

© 2015 Scholastic Education International (S) Pte Ltd ISBN 978-981-4629-63-8

A **MOMENT** later, Uncle Stingysnout awakened me with a bucket of **ice-cold** water in the snout.

"**Wake up**, Geronimo!" he squeaked. "I'm counting on you to refurbish the castle **INSIDE AND OUT**. And when I say **INSIDE AND OUT**, I really mean **INSIDE AND OUT**. This is my very **Last** request!"

"B-but, Uncle —" I began, but he cut me off.

"Oh, poor, poor me!" he moaned. "I'm so **old** and so **sick**, and I just have this one **TINY** last request before I croak, which might be **very**, **very** soon! You'll help me out, won't you, Nephew?"

MOLDY MOZZARELLA! This time, I knew I couldn't do it **alone**. It was too much **WORK**! It would take me an entire year to **refurbish the castle** inside and out.

3 What do you think Geronimo is going to do?

(Originally published in Italy by Edizioni Piemme Ma che vacanza...a Rocca Taccagna!) Excerpt from *The Stinky Cheese Vacation*

Circle the correct answers.

1. What do you think is the real reason Uncle Stingysnout wanted Geronimo to refurbish the castle instead of getting a contractor?

    (a)   He did not know where to get a good contractor.

    (b)   Contractors could not be trusted.

    (c)   He knew that Geronimo would be able to do a better job.

    (d)   He did not want to spend any money and wanted Geronimo to do it for free.

2. Why do you think Geronimo FAINTED?

    (a)   The list of things was so long, Geronimo fainted from the shock.

    (b)   Geronimo fainted because the castle was old and stinky.

    (c)   Geronimo was being strangled by the long list.

    (d)   Geronimo was so hungry from all the work he did and had no more energy.

3. What did Geronimo's uncle mean by the phrase, "before I croak!"?

    (a)   He means that he would soon start croaking like a frog.

    (b)   He is referring to the curse that would turn him into a frog.

    (c)   He means, before he dies.

    (d)   He means that he would soon be unable to speak.

4. Why does Geronimo think it would take him a whole year to refurbish the castle?

    (a)   The castle was too big and it would take him a long time to walk through all the rooms.

    (b)   There were too many things to do.

    (c)   That was all the time that he had to work on the castle.

    (d)   He could only leave his job for one year to help his uncle.

5. Why do you think Geronimo was leaning against the freezer when he woke up?

    (a)   His bedroom was next to the kitchen.

    (b)   He had been feeling hot.

    (c)   He had been leaning against the freezer when he fell asleep.

    (d)   Geronimo liked to sleep while standing up.

 Excerpt from *The Stinky Cheese Vacation*
(Originally published in Italy by Edizioni Piemme Ma che vacanza...a Rocca Taccagna!)   © 2015 Scholastic Education International (S) Pte Ltd ISBN 978-981-4629-63-8

Look at the picture of the castle. Here are some of the things that were done to refurbish the castle.

1. Restore the roof.
2. Fix the electrical system.
3. Clean the windows.
4. Paint the walls.
5. Clear the moat.
6. Mow the grass.
7. Fix the bridge and the pathways.
8. Repair the cracks in the walls.

Match each of the tasks to the correct picture. Write the correct number.

Excerpt from The Stinky Cheese Vacation
(Originally published in Italy by Edizioni Piemme *Ma che vacanza...a Rocca Taccagna!*)

Uncle Stingysnout — the Cheapest Rodent on Mouse Island

Uncle Stingysnout really is the cheapest rodent on Mouse Island. Look at some of the things he does to save money. Why do you think he does them? Complete each sentence with a reason. Use the phrases below.

- so that he could save his breath
- so it does not get used up
- so that he would not have to buy wood
- so that he can save water by not bathing
- so that he can save money on electricity
- so he does not have to buy new tea bags

1 He washes his hands with barely any soap _____

2 He reuses the tea bags when making tea _____

3 When it rains, he doesn't use an umbrella _____

Excerpt from *The Stinky Cheese Vacation*
(Originally published in Italy by Edizioni Piemme *Ma che vacanza...a Rocca Taccagna!*)

© 2015 Scholastic Education International (S) Pte Ltd   ISBN 978-981-4629-63-8

4 He learnt to be stingy from his great-grandfather who barely

spoke _____

5 He painted flames on the fireplace

_____

_____

6 He reads by the light of lightning

_____

_____

Excerpt from *The Stinky Cheese Vacation*
(Originally published in Italy by Edizioni Piemme *Ma che vacanza...a Rocca Taccagna*)

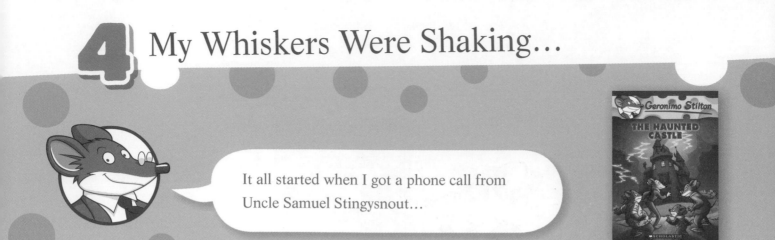

It all started when I got a phone call from Uncle Samuel Stingysnout...

"Geronimo!" Uncle Samuel shouted. "I'm calling to invite you to **Penny Pincher Castle** for the **ceremony** that will take place on October thirty-first. Will you come or not?"

I didn't have a clue what he was talking about. "What **ceremony**?" I asked.

"You know, the **ceremony**, Geronimo!" he yelled. **"THE C-E-R-E-M-O-N-Y!"**

"Yes, I heard you, but what **ceremony** are you squeaking about?" I asked, trying to be polite.

"GERONIMO!" he hollered. **"ALL** the relatives are coming! The only one who won't be there is **YOU**!"

I was starting to lose my patience. "But what is this **ceremony**?"

He continued as though I hadn't spoken. "Plus I've **organized** everything! You wouldn't want me to **waste** all that effort, would you?" Before I could get a squeak in edgewise, he went on, "So it's all settled, then. I will expect you, **Benjamin**, **THEA**, and **Trap** for the **ceremony**. . . ."

At that point, my whiskers were shaking with exasperation. **"WHAT CEREMONY???"** I shrieked.

 **Chew on it!**

1. What words tell you how Uncle Samuel was speaking to Geronimo?

2. What do you think the ceremony is about?

Excerpt from *The Haunted Castle*
(Originally published in Italy by Edizioni Piemme *Ritorno a Rocca Taccagna*)

© 2015 Scholastic Education International (S) Pte Ltd ISBN 978-981-4629-63-8

That was when we got cut off.

It was all so **strange**! You see, the relationship between the *Stilton* family and the **Stingysnout** family is strained, for one simple reason: The Stingysnouts are a bit **stingy**.

If you look up the word *stingy* in the DICTIONARY, you'll find this definition:

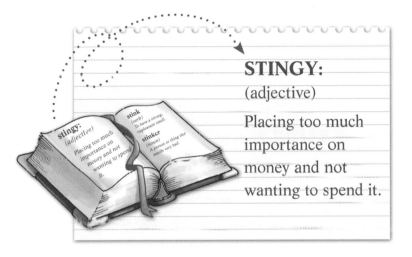

STINGY:

(adjective)

Placing too much importance on money and not wanting to spend it.

I told my sister THEA, my cousin **trap**, and my nephew **Benjamin** that we had been invited to Penny Pincher Castle. These were their reactions:

3. Would you enjoy a visit to Penny Pincher Castle? Why?

"I don't want to go to Penny Pincher Castle! It's colder than iced cheese there — all because Uncle Samuel won't spend the money to turn on the heat."

"I don't want to go to Penny Pincher Castle! there's never anything to eat there — all because Uncle Samuel won't spend the money to put cheese in the fridge."

"I don't want to go to Penny Pincher Castle! It's so dark and spooky there — all because Uncle Samuel won't spend the money to turn on the lights."

Excerpt from *The Haunted Castle*
(Originally published in Italy by Edizioni Piemme *Ritorno a Rocca Taccagna*)

Circle the correct answers.

1. What can you tell about Uncle Samuel from this passage?

    (a) He likes to plan family parties all the time.

    (b) He is Geronimo's favorite uncle.

    (c) He dislikes Geronimo.

    (d) He speaks loudly and is not a good listener.

2. Why were Geronimo's whiskers "shaking with exasperation"?

    (a) Uncle Samuel was not listening to him.

    (b) Geronimo was very excited about the ceremony.

    (c) It was cold in the room and Geronimo was shivering.

    (d) Geronimo hates going to ceremonies.

3. What word means the opposite of **stingy**?

    (a) Ungenerous

    (b) Grateful

    (c) Generous

    (d) Plentiful

4. How did the telephone conversation end?

    (a) Suddenly and unexpectedly

    (b) Both parties said a pleasant goodbye.

    (c) Geronimo switched off the phone.

    (d) Uncle Samuel slammed down the phone.

5. What was so "**strange**"?

    (a) Geronimo had no idea what Uncle Samuel was talking about.

    (b) The invitation to the ceremony was strange because the families did not get along well with one another.

    (c) The phone call getting cut off

    (d) Uncle Samuel shouting at Geronimo

Excerpt from *The Haunted Castle*
(Originally published in Italy by Edizioni Piemme *Ritorno a Rocca Taccagna*)

© 2015 Scholastic Education International (S) Pte Ltd ISBN 978-981-4629-63-8

Geronimo told THEA, Trap, and Benjamin that they had been invited to Penny Pincher Castle. Read their reactions. Complete the description of Penny Pincher Castle with the words or phrases in the box.

put cheese	too cold	dark	spooky
turn on the lights	turn on the heat	nothing to eat	

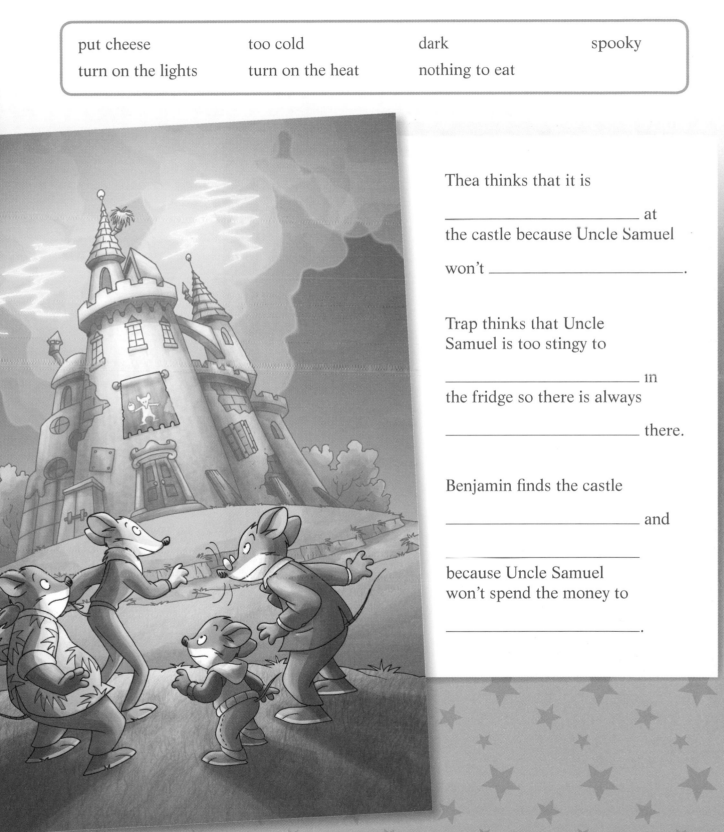

Thea thinks that it is

_____ at the castle because Uncle Samuel

won't _____.

Trap thinks that Uncle Samuel is too stingy to

_____ in the fridge so there is always

_____ there.

Benjamin finds the castle

_____ and

_____

because Uncle Samuel won't spend the money to

_____.

Excerpt from *The Haunted Castle*
(Originally published in Italy by Edizioni Piemme *Ritorno a Rocca Taccagna*)

The Stingysnout Family and the Stiltons are very different. Let me tell you more about the Stingysnouts.

Chew on it!

The Stingysnout Family

The Stingysnouts come from the Valley of Lack, where the ancestral family home, Penny Pincher Castle, is located on top of Cheap Change Hill. For years, Uncle Samuel has lived there with his son, Stevie, and his younger sister, Chintzina.

Years and years ago, Samuel's great-grandfather, Cheddar Cheapskate Stingysnout, married Serena Stilton, Geronimo's great-grandmother. Despite being distantly related, the two families do not get along — mostly because the Stingysnouts are so cheap! The Stiltons and the Stingysnouts see each other only during family ceremonies, like weddings and funerals.

1. How do you think the Stiltons feel about the Stingysnouts?

Excerpt from *The Haunted Castle*
(Originally published in Italy by Edizioni Piemme Ritorno a Rocca Taccagna)

Samuel Stingysnout

The head of the Stingysnout family, Samuel, is a real master of frugality. His motto is "I need to set an example for the other Stingysnouts!" He prides himself on finding new (and often extreme) ways to save money. He's been known to wake before dawn so he can sneak over to his neighbor's house to read his newspaper instead of buying his own.

Samuel washes himself without soap so he doesn't have to purchase any. He refuses to spend money on toilet paper, and some family members believe he's been wearing the same pair of underwear for more than a decade. He even wears pants inside out so he doesn't have to wash them!

When Samuel makes tea, he dips the tea bag in the water for a second — PLUNK — and then he takes it out right away. "This way tea bags can last for years and years," he tells anyone who will listen. But perhaps his cheapest (and grossest) habit is this: After he brushes his fur, he pulls stray whiskers out of the comb and uses them as dental floss. Eww!

2. How does wearing the same thing over and over without washing it save money?

3. What do you think of Samuel Stingysnout?

Excerpt from *The Haunted Castle*
(Originally published in Italy by Edizioni Piemme *Ritorno a Rocca Taccagna*)

Meet The Stingysnout Family

Circle the correct answers.

1. How many mice live at Penny Pincher Castle?

    (a) 5

    (b) 3

    (c) 1

    (d) Too many mice who use up precious energy and money.

2. The Stingysnouts "are so cheap!" What does this mean?

    (a) They are stingy and will not spend any money if they can help it.

    (b) They don't like to see the Stiltons wasting money.

    (c) They are poor and like cheap things.

    (d) They will only spend money on close relatives.

3. Do the Stingysnouts and Stiltons see each other often?

    (a) No, only on special occasions.

    (b) Yes.

    (c) Not as much as Geronimo would like

    (d) Depends on whether the Stiltons are free

4. What is a "motto"?

    (a) A very cheap car

    (b) A belief that you say and live out

    (c) Something you say to your family

    (d) Something you are very good at doing

5. Why is Uncle Samuel the head of the Stingysnout family?

    (a) He is the most stingy and frugal mouse in the family.

    (b) He has the best and most gross ideas for saving money.

    (c) He lives in Penny Pincher Castle and whoever lives there gets to be the head of the family.

    (d) He is the oldest member of the family still alive.

Excerpt from *The Haunted Castle*
(Originally published in Italy by Edizioni Piemme *Ritorno a Rocca Taccagna*)

© 2015 Scholastic Education International (S) Pte Ltd ISBN 978-981-4629-63-8

Meet The Stingysnout Family

Uncle Samuel has many ways of saving money. Complete Uncle Samuel's list below.

Method 1	Wake up before dawn to sneak over to my neighbor's house to _____ so I do not have to buy my own.
Method 2	Wash myself _____ so I do not have to buy any.
Method 3	Do not buy _____ and wear the same pair of _____ for as long as I can.
Method 4	Wear my _____ inside out so I do not have to _____.
Method 5	Re-use _____ so I can make many cups of tea with one tea bag.
Method 6	Use the stray whiskers from my fur as _____.

How can you be *stingy* at home and at school?
Think of more ways to be stingier than Uncle Samuel!

© 2015 Scholastic Education International (S) Pte Ltd ISBN 978-981-4629-63-8

Excerpt from *The Haunted Castle*
(Originally published in Italy by Edizioni Piemme *Ritorno a Rocca Taccagna*)

6 Night Frights!

At Penny Pincher Castle, on a dark, stormy night, things are not what they seem…

I tried to **sleep**, but I couldn't. I was **TOO AFRAID**!

It was a dark and stormy night. **LIGHTNING BOLTS** lit up the windows and cast **SPOOKY** shadows over the room. The wind whistled and seemed to whisper: **BIGWIG… BIGWIIIIIG… BIIIIIIGWIIIIIG…**

I decided to go down to the kitchen to make myself some hot tea. Maybe I wouldn't be so terrified if I had a nice, full belly.

I tiptoed down the **CREAKY** staircase, feeling my way carefully, because I didn't have a candle. I was almost glad of the darkness . . . who knows what horrors would have been visible if it had been light?

At last, I arrived in the kitchen. Thank goodness!

Just then, I heard someone pawing around behind the corner — and a **monstrous** shadow appeared on the wall! A huge, threatening paw was reaching for me! It looked like the claw of an enormouse cat!

Chew on it!

1. Why was Geronimo tiptoeing?

Excerpt from *The Haunted Castle*
(Originally published in Italy by Edizioni Piemme *Ritorno a Rocca Taccagna*)
© 2015 Scholastic Education International (S) Pte Ltd   ISBN 978-981-4629-63-8

"Wh-who's there?" I cried.

What could it be?

From behind the corner, out popped — **THEA**, **Trap**, and **Benjamin**!

"Huh? You're here, too?" they **YELPED**.

"Huh? You're here, too?" I **YELPED**.

"We wanted to make some hot **tea**," my sister explained.

It turned out making hot **tea** was easier said than done! We looked through all the cupboards and found only *one* tea bag, which, naturally, had been used!

While we **HEATED** up the water, I decided to confide in my family. "There's something **bizarre** about that coffin. It is way too light. It's very **strange**!"

"Hmm, well, why don't we go **check it out**?" Thea suggested. That's my sister for you. She's totally fearless!

I **shuddered** at the thought. The idea of touching that *thing* made my fur stand **on end**.

But not Thea's. She **scurried** into the room with the **coffin**. She felt around in the dark until she found it. Then she lifted the cover and cried out, "**IT'S EMPTYYYYYYYYYY!**"

2. Who or what was the monstrous shadow?

3. What do you think they would find in the coffin? Why?

Excerpt from *The Haunted Castle* (Originally published in Italy by Edizioni Piemme *Ritorno a Rocca Taccagna*)

Night Frights!

Circle the correct answers.

1. Why did Geronimo go to the kitchen?

    (a)   He was too afraid to stay in his room.

    (b)   He thought filling his tummy would make him less afraid so he could sleep.

    (c)   He was hoping to find someone to talk to about the coffin.

    (d)   He wanted to check out the coffin and solve the mystery.

2. What is a "night fright", as mentioned in the title?

    (a)   The sound the wind makes during a storm

    (b)   Someone who is frightened of the dark

    (c)   Scary things in the night

    (d)   Creatures that fight at night

3. The teabag "naturally, had been used!" What does this tell us?

    (a)   Geronimo expected the tea bag to be used.

    (b)   The teabag was made from natural ingredients.

    (c)   Naturally used tea bags are the best for hot tea.

    (d)   The rest of the tea bags had not been used.

4. What does "confide" mean?

    (a)   To chat with someone quietly

    (b)   To have a conversation with your family

    (c)   To have confidence in your family

    (d)   To tell someone a secret and trust them not to tell anyone else

5. What "horrors" was Geronimo afraid of seeing?

    (a)   Ghosts and other monsters

    (b)   Uncle Samuel

    (c)   Shadows caused by light

    (d)   Spiders, bats and rats scurrying about

 Excerpt from *The Haunted Castle*
(Originally published in Italy by Edizioni Piemme *Ritorno a Rocca Taccagna*)   © 2015 Scholastic Education International (S) Pte Ltd ISBN 978-981-4629-63-8

Night  Frights!

What was Geronimo's room like? Look at a picture of his room below. Complete the labels with the words in the box.

dark	lightning bolts	candles	shadows
leaking	windows	curtains	windy

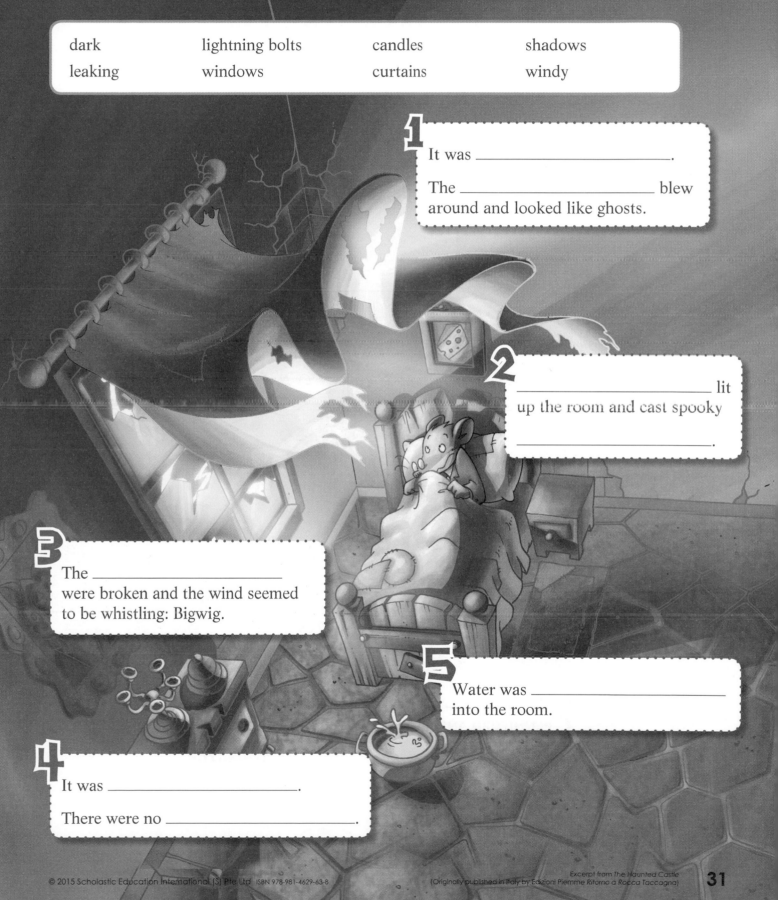

1

It was _____.

The _____ blew around and looked like ghosts.

2

_____ lit up the room and cast spooky

_____.

3

The _____ were broken and the wind seemed to be whistling: Bigwig.

5

Water was _____ into the room.

4

It was _____.

There were no _____.

© 2015 Scholastic Education International (S) Pte Ltd ISBN 978-981-4629-63-8

Excerpt from *The Haunted Castle* (Originally published in Italy by Edizioni Piemme Ritorno a Rocca Taccagna)

The Stingysnout Family

Write the correct word(s) to complete the description of each Stingysnout.

neighbor's newspapers

soaps

three

free samples

taking one lick at a time

shoes

fat-free cheese

ancient sculptures

steel

recycles old bedsheets

save her breath

energy

heat

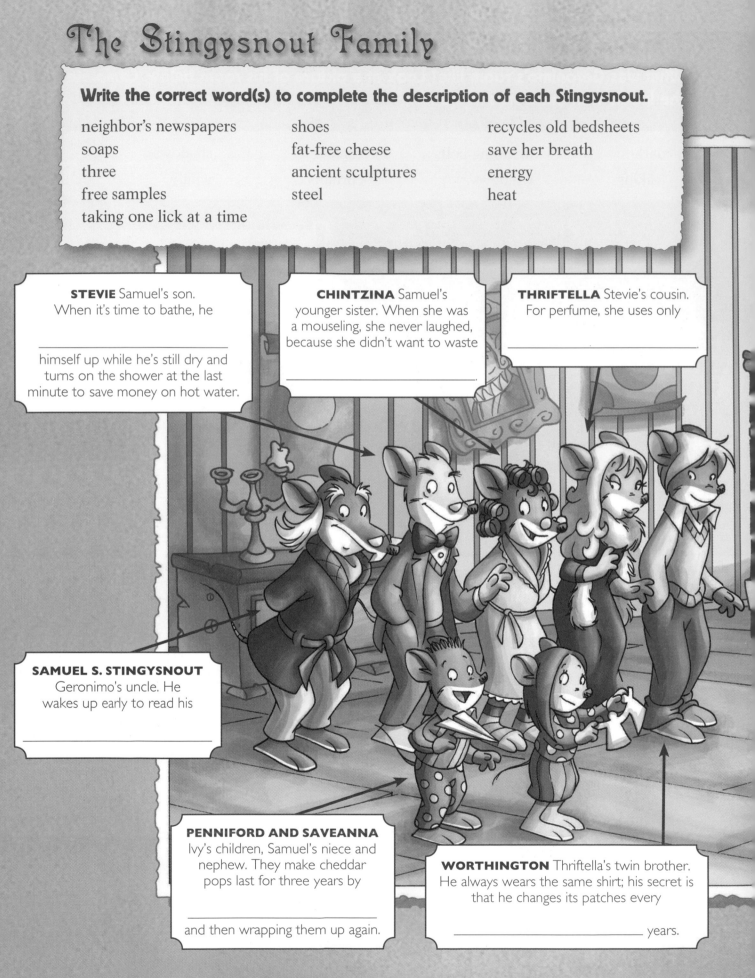

STEVIE Samuel's son. When it's time to bathe, he

_____ himself up while he's still dry and turns on the shower at the last minute to save money on hot water.

CHINTZINA Samuel's younger sister. When she was a mouseling, she never laughed, because she didn't want to waste

_____.

THRIFTELLA Stevie's cousin. For perfume, she uses only

_____

SAMUEL S. STINGYSNOUT Geronimo's uncle. He wakes up early to read his

_____

PENNIFORD AND SAVEANNA Ivy's children, Samuel's niece and nephew. They make cheddar pops last for three years by

_____ and then wrapping them up again.

WORTHINGTON Thriftella's twin brother. He always wears the same shirt; his secret is that he changes its patches every

_____ years.

Excerpt from *The Haunted Castle*
(Originally published in Italy by Edizioni Piemme *Ritorno a Rocca Taccagna*)

© 2015 Scholastic Education International (S) Pte Ltd ISBN 978-981-4629-63-8

FRUGELLA Michael's sister and Samuel's cousin. She eats only

_____

so she can save calories.

IVY Samuel's daughter. She doesn't pronounce double letters so she can

_____

She's the spitting image of her father.

MICHAEL MISERMOUSE Samuel's cousin and an antiques dealer. He sells old bread crusts, passing them off as

_____

HOARDEN ACCOUNTS Ivy's husband. In the winter, he wears three pairs of long underwear so he doesn't have to turn the

_____ on.

ZELDA Stevie's journalist cousin. She wears shoes with heels made of

_____

so they don't wear out.

GRANDMA CHEAPERLY Samuel's mother. She

_____

to make her blouses.

GRANDPA CHEAPERLY Samuel's father. He always leaves the house in slippers so he doesn't wear out the soles of his

_____

Excerpt from *The Haunted Castle*
(Originally published in Italy by Edizioni Piemme *Ritorno a Rocca Taccagna*)

Spring is finally here and I'm out and about in the lovely weather.

Chew on it!

1. What do you think the weather was like?

It was a beautiful Saturday afternoon in *spring*, and I was whistling *HAPPILY* as I strolled along the streets of New Mouse City. I was in a good mood because I'd planned a really nice day. First, I'd shop for some fresh cheese, then I'd head over to **New Mouse City's library**, where the library mouse was holding a **book** for me. It was something I'd wanted to read for a **LONG** time.

When I was done with my shopping, I scurried over to the library. After chatting with the library mouse, I checked out the book.

The security guard shouted, **"The library is closing!** All rodents are kindly asked to get their books and leave the premises!"

I scampered onto the elevator and pushed the down . The elevator began going down. But suddenly, between the third and second floors, I heard a **SCREECH**, and the elevator came to a dead **STOP**. The lights went out, and I was plunged into **DARKNESS**.

 Excerpt from *I'm Not a Supermouse!*
(Originally published in Italy by Edizioni Piemme *Non Sono un Supertopo!*)

 ISBN 978-981-4629-63-8

A Mouse Trap

I waited for a moment, then squeaked at the top of my lungs: "Help! The **elevator** is stuck!"

There was no response. A **chill** ran down my tail as a **TERRIFYING** thought struck me: "I'm stuck in an elevator on a Saturday afternoon and no one has a clue I'm here!"

Cold **sweat** dripped from my whiskers. My head was spinning like a **mousey-go-round** at an amusement park. My heart was racing **FASTER** than a gerbil on a treadmill. I banged my paws on the steel doors, screaming, "**HELP**, I'm traaaapppped!"

Despite the **darkness**, I saw something move. "**AAAAAAAAARRRRRRGGHH!**" I screeched.

Then I looked closer: It was only my own **REFLECTION** in the elevator's mirror!

2. What would you do if you were stuck in an elevator?

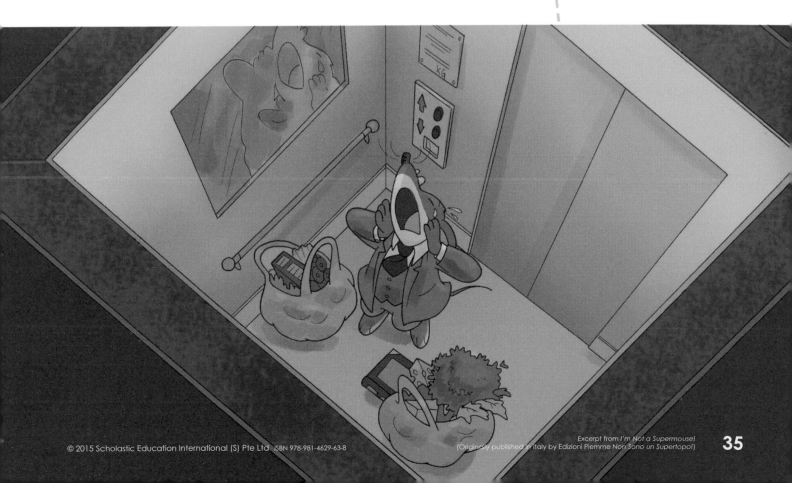

Excerpt from *I'm Not a Supermouse!*
(Originally published in Italy by Edizioni Piemme *Non Sono un Supertopo!*)

 **Circle the correct answers.**

1. Why was Geronimo in a good mood?

    (a)   It was the weekend and he intended to do nice things.

    (b)   Whistling and walking made him happy.

    (c)   He was going to have an adventure.

    (d)   He was going to read a long book.

2. The security guard shouted **"The library is closing!"**. What did he expect those in the library to do?

    (a)   He expected them to get stuck in the elevator.

    (b)   He expected them to stay in the library.

    (c)   He expected them to leave the library.

    (d)   He expected them to look for him.

3. Why was Geronimo terrified that he was stuck in an elevator on a Saturday?

    (a)   The library was haunted.

    (b)   His fresh cheese would melt in the elevator and be wasted.

    (c)   He was afraid of heights and elevators.

    (d)   No one will rescue him until Monday because the library is closed on Sundays.

4. Geronimo felt cold **sweat**, his head spun, and his heart raced? What was happening to him?

    (a)   He was very hot and having a headache.

    (b)   He was afraid and panicking.

    (c)   He was out of breath from shouting for help.

    (d)   It was very cold and chilly in the elevator.

5. What floor in the library do you think Geronimo was on?

    (a)   4th floor

    (b)   2nd floor

    (c)   Ground floor

    (d)   Rooftop

Excerpt from *I'm Not a Supermouse!*
(Originally published in Italy by Edizioni Piemme *Non Sono un Supertopo!*)

© 2015 Scholastic Education International (S) Pte Ltd ISBN 978-981-4629-63-8

A Mouse Trap

Geronimo was stuck in the elevator. Look at what he had with him. What do you think he did? Use the words to complete the passage. He rummaged through his shopping bag....

love	darkness	lucky	dark
sip	wait	cheese	pitch

.... and found a piece of 1. _____.
I began munching on it slowly, then drank a

2. _____ of orange juice. It was

3. _____ I'd just done
my shopping: a piece of cheese usually calms me
down right away. After all, what mouse doesn't

4. _____ cheese?

Too bad it was so 5. _____ in

here! In fact, it was 6. _____

black. All that 7. _____ reminded
me that I hate small spaces. I get really claustrophobic!

I took a deep breath. There was nothing to do but

8. _____.

If you were stuck in an elevator for a long time, what would you like to have with you?

_____

_____

Excerpt from *I'm Not a Supermouse!*
(Originally published in Italy by Edizioni Piemme *Non Sono un Supertopo!*)

8 I Thought I'd Leave My Fur There!

I escaped from the elevator.
The next day, back in the office…

Chew on it!

The next day, I told everybody in the office about my **unlucky** adventure. Oh, excuse me, I almost forgot to tell you — I run *The Rodent's Gazette,* the biggest newspaper in New Mouse City.

"I was so scared!" I sighed. "Alone all night in the elevator, in the dark. . . . I thought I'd leave my FUR there forever!"

My sister THEA snorted. "No chance of leaving **anything** there, except maybe your common sense! You just spent a night in an elevator, that's all!"

"If it were me, I would have just taken a nice ratnap," my cousin Trap snickered. "If life gives you cheese, make a triple-decker sandwich! Know what I mean?"

Bruce was quiet. He put a paw on me and said seriously, "Tell me, Cheesehead, why didn't you call me right away?"

"Actually . . . hmm . . . I didn't think of it," I admitted. "I don't know why."

1. What does Geronimo mean by "leave my FUR there forever"?

Excerpt from I'm Not a Supermouse! (Originally published in Italy by Edizioni Piemme Non Sono un Supertopo!)

Bruce **nodded**. Then he shouted in my ear: "I'll tell you why, **Cheese Puff**! Because you're a **BUNDLE** of nerves! Because you **LOST YOUR COOL**! Because you panicked!"

He **pinched** my ear. "OUUUCCHHH!" I shrieked.

Bruce ignored me. "Remember these **golden** rules:

> RULE NO. 1: ALWAYS KEEP CALM!
> RULE NO. 2: BE QUICK ON YOUR PAWS!
> RULE NO. 3: LEARN TO ADAPT!
> RULE NO. 4: BE AWARE OF YOUR SURROUNDINGS!

"Got it, **CHAMP**?"

He **scribbled** something in a small orange notebook, then slammed it shut. He nodded, gave my sister a **high five** (why?), **WINKED** at my cousin (why?), and **signaled** Benjamin not to worry (why, why, why?).

Bruce turned to look me in the snout. "I've got just the **cure** for what ails you," he declared. "*Just you wait!*"

Bruce grabbed my tail and dragged me up the stairs to the roof. An orange **helicopter** was waiting for us.

2. Why do you think Bruce pinched Geronimo's ear?

3. What do you think is going to happen to Geronimo?

© 2015 Scholastic Education International (S) Pte Ltd ISBN 978-981-4629-63-8

(Originally published in Italy by Edizioni Piemme Non Sono un Supertopo!)

Excerpt from *I'm Not a Supermouse!*

I Thought I'd Leave My Fur There!

Circle the correct answers.

1. Thea "snorted" and Trap "**snickered**". What did they think of Geronimo's unlucky adventure in the elevator?

    (a) They thought it was quite funny.

    (b) Being stuck in an elevator happens all the time and is no big deal as long as you have food to eat.

    (c) It was no big deal to be trapped in an elevator and he should have just made the best of the situation.

    (d) They were bored with Geronimo's story.

2. What is the problem with Geronimo?

    (a) He worries a lot and is scared easily.

    (b) He works too hard and has no hobbies.

    (c) He is afraid of the dark.

    (d) He is not very intelligent.

3. Why didn't Geronimo call Bruce for help?

    (a) He did not know Bruce's number.

    (b) He was worried Bruce would pinch his ear when he was rescued.

    (c) He panicked and was not thinking properly.

    (d) No one knows.

4. What kind of mouse is Bruce?

    (a) A violent and unfriendly mouse

    (b) A mouse with dangerous rules

    (c) A mouse that likes golden things

    (d) The opposite of Geronimo

5. What does "If life gives you cheese, make a triple-decker **sandwich**!" mean?

    (a) A triple-decker sandwich is Trap's and Geronimo's favorite sandwich.

    (b) Trap hopes there will be lots of cheese in his life.

    (c) When Trap takes naps he dreams of triple-decker sandwiches.

    (d) It means to make the most of a bad situation and turn it into something good.

 Excerpt from *I'm Not a Supermouse!*
(Originally published in Italy by Edizioni Piemme *Non Sono un Supertopo!*) © 2015 Scholastic Education International (S) Pte Ltd ISBN 978-981-4629-63-8

Bruce has golden rules to get him out of difficult situations.

> RULE NO. 1: ALWAYS KEEP CALM!
> RULE NO. 2: BE QUICK ON YOUR PAWS!
> RULE NO. 3: LEARN TO ADAPT!
> RULE NO. 4: BE AWARE OF YOUR SURROUNDINGS!

Geronimo too has his own golden rules for what to do.

What do you think they are? Use the words to help you.

RUN AWAY   SCREAM LOUDLY   CHEESE   DANGEROUS

RULE NO. 1: _____ WHEN YOU CAN.

RULE NO. 2: _____ FOR HELP IF IN DANGER.

RULE NO. 3: NEVER LEAVE HOME WITHOUT _____.

RULE NO. 4: DO NOT DO ANYTHING _____.

Can you add two more rules for Geronimo?

RULE NO. 5: _____

RULE NO. 6: _____

Excerpt from *I'm Not a Supermouse!*
(Originally published in Italy by Edizioni Piemme *Non Sono un Supertopo!*)

9 A Place With Lots and Lots of Sand

Find out more about where part of my adventure with Bruce takes place. A place with lots and lots of…

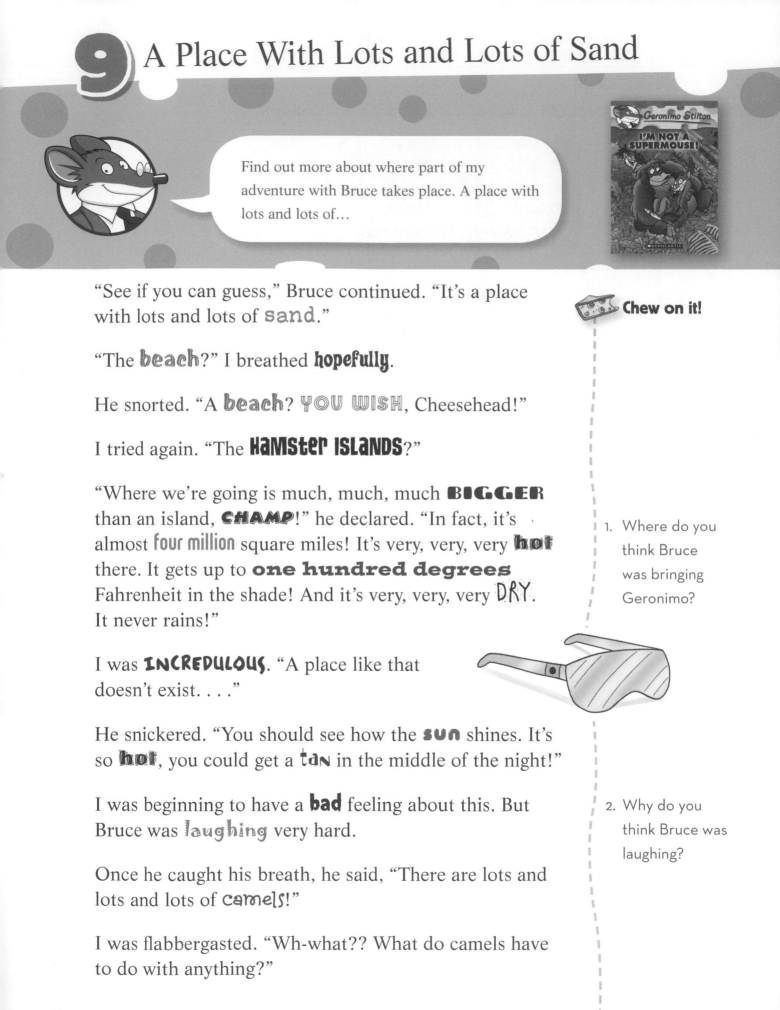

"See if you can guess," Bruce continued. "It's a place with lots and lots of sand."

"The beach?" I breathed hopefully.

He snorted. "A beach? YOU WISH, Cheesehead!"

I tried again. "The HAMSTER ISLANDS?"

"Where we're going is much, much, much BIGGER than an island, CHAMP!" he declared. "In fact, it's almost four million square miles! It's very, very, very hot there. It gets up to one hundred degrees Fahrenheit in the shade! And it's very, very, very DRY. It never rains!"

I was INCREDULOUS. "A place like that doesn't exist. . . ."

He snickered. "You should see how the sun shines. It's so hot, you could get a tan in the middle of the night!"

I was beginning to have a bad feeling about this. But Bruce was laughing very hard.

Once he caught his breath, he said, "There are lots and lots and lots of camels!"

I was flabbergasted. "Wh-what?? What do camels have to do with anything?"

Chew on it!

1. Where do you think Bruce was bringing Geronimo?

2. Why do you think Bruce was laughing?

Excerpt from *I'm Not a Supermouse!*
(Originally published in Italy by Edizioni Piemme *Non Sono un Supertopo!*)

© 2015 Scholastic Education International (S) Pte Ltd ISBN 978-981-4629-63-8

Bruce was **rolling with laughter** in the helicopter, making it **BOUNCE** up and down. I clutched my stomach. You see, I have a bad history of **MOTION SICKNESS**.

"Look down," Bruce sputtered between laughs. "There are the **camels**!"

Below us was a blanket of sand. It was veryveryvery **big** . . . veryveryvery **hot** . . . and veryveryvery **dry** . . . with lots and lots and lots of **camels**!

Bruce had finally gotten control of himself. "I bet you're wondering where the **beach** is, right?" He burst out laughing again.

But that was no **beach**. It was **the SaharA DesErt**!

"If you don't lather yourself up with sunblock from the tip of your **tail** to the tip of your **whiskers**, you'll be in agony!" he bellowed. "Out here, you need a sunblock that's **SPF 1000**!"

"But **SPF 1000** sunblock doesn't exist!" I stammered.

"Exaaaaaaaactly! So stay in the **SHADE** as much as you can, otherwise you'll be a **ROASTED RODENT**!

Excerpt from *I'm Not a Supermouse!*
(Originally published in Italy by Edizioni Piemme *Non Sono un Supertopo!*)

Circle the correct answers.

1. Where did Geronimo hope to go?

    (a) The beach

    (b) The Sahara Desert

    (c) A helicopter

    (d) An island

2. Why do you think Bruce said, "A **beach**? **YOU WISH**, Cheesehead!"?

    (a) He was trying to grant Geronimo his wish.

    (b) He was hinting to Geronimo that their destination would not be such a nice place.

    (c) He was asking Geronimo to make a wish.

    (d) He was asking Geronimo to help him decide where to go.

3. Why did Geronimo clutch his stomach?

    (a) He was starting to feel sick from the motion.

    (b) He needed to use the toilet.

    (c) He was laughing so hard his stomach hurt.

    (d) He was in shock.

4. What did Bruce advise Geronimo to do in the **DesErt**?

    (a) To get ready to be roasted

    (b) To stay in the shade as much as he could

    (c) To get a tan in the middle of the night

    (d) To look down instead of up

5. What was Bruce suggesting about the **SaharA DesErt** when he said "Out here, you need a sunblock that's **SPF 1000**!"?

    (a) That the Sahara Desert is very cool

    (b) That Geronimo would enjoy being in the Sahara Desert

    (c) That the Sahara Desert is extremely hot

    (d) That there was not much shade in the Sahara Desert

 Excerpt from *I'm Not a Supermouse!*
(Originally published in Italy by Edizioni Piemme *Non Sono un Supertopo!*) ISBN 978-981-4629-63-8

What is the Sahara Desert like? Complete the leaflet below with information from the text.

The Sahara

The Sahara is the largest _____ in the world. It is almost

_____ square miles. It is very _____

there and can get up to _____ Fahrenheit even in the shade.

It is a place with lots and lots of _____ It is very

_____ because it never rains there.

There are a lot of _____ that live in the desert and they are often used by the nomads for transportation.

Survival Gear

Bruce took Geronimo to the Sahara Desert and then to the North Pole! He told him to pack survival gear for the trip to both of these places. List the items correctly.

BANDAGES FOR BLISTERS

BREATHABLE WATERPROOF JACKET

BARRIER SKIN CREAM*

HIKING BOOTS

EARMUFFS

ENERGY BARS

FLASHLIGHT

GLASSES FOR THE WIND, FOG, AND SUN

HEAVY SCARF

HIKING BOOTS

HEAVY WOOL SOCKS

SNOWSHOES

DESERT SURVIVAL GEAR

Excerpt from I'm Not a Supermouse!
(Originally published in Italy by Edizioni Piemme Non Sono un Supertopo!)

© 2015 Scholastic Education International (S) Pte Ltd   ISBN 978-981-4629-63-8

SNAKE AND SCORPION ANTIVENOM KIT

BREATHABLE WATERPROOF PANTS

THERMOS

SUNBLOCK

TRIPLE-LAYER WOOL SWEATER

SNOUT MASK WITH INSULATED LINING

MIRRORED SUNGLASSES

SUN HAT

WATER BOTTLE AND DRINK MIX

WATERPROOF TAIL COVER

LINED GLOVES

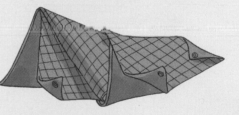

THERMAL TENT

NORTH POLE SURVIVAL KIT

Excerpt from *I'm Not a Superhero!*
(Originally published in Italy by Edizioni Piemme *Non Sono un Supertopo!*)

I promised my nephew Benjamin to throw a Halloween party at my house, so we had some shopping to do for the party.

I took Benjamin to **TRICKS FOR TAILS**, the most popular party store in New Mouse City. It has lots of decorations, **weird** gadgets, and party pranks.

When we entered the store, we were greeted by the owner, **Paws Prankster**. One thing you should know about **Paws**: He loves to test out his pranks on unsuspecting customers.

Of course, today was no exception.

"Like my ring?" he giggled, waving his paw in my face.

I took a closer look, and a stream of **water** squirted me in the snout!

Cheese niblets!

"Got ya!" **Paws** guffawed.

"Look at this, Uncle," Benjamin said, pointing to a **humongous** orange pumpkin.

I had to admit it was pretty impressive.

But why had someone left a **banana peel** on top of the pumpkin? How **strange**!

Benjamin found a rack with lots of scary costumes.

Chew on it!

1. What do you think Paws Prankster would do?

2. What kind of costume was Benjamin likely to get?

Excerpt from *The Peculiar Pumpkin Thief*
(Originally published in Italy by Edizioni Piemme *Lo strano caso della Torre Pagliaccia*)

© 2015 Scholastic Education International (S) Pte Ltd   ISBN 978-981-4629-63-8

He tried on a **GHOST**, an **ALIEN**, and a **SKELETON** costume.

They were all so **SPOOKY**, we couldn't decide. We decided to think it over and come back in a few days.

We were about to leave when I felt someone — or something — tug on my **tail**.

I turned around, but there was no one there. **How odd!**

I took another step. Again I felt a tug on my **tail**.

I whirled around fast, but still no one was there. **How weird!**

A rubber bat dangling from the ceiling stared at me with evil eyes. **YIKES!** I was beginning to get the creeps.

At that moment, the giant pumpkin began to move.

"**Yoo-hoo!**" a voice whispered.

Suddenly, a furry gray snout popped out of the pumpkin.

"Like my little **joke**, Stilton?" the mouse giggled.

I should have known. It was my friend **Hercule Poirat**, the famouse detective. Hercule loves to play pranks, and he's always eating **bananas**.

"Stilton, I could really use your help solving a **HALLOWEEN MYSTERY**...." he began.

But I cut him off.

Hercule loved to get me to help with his crazy cases, but I wasn't about to get involved. I had a **HALLOWEEN** party to plan!

3. What do you think Geronimo would do?

© 2015 Scholastic Education International (S) Pte Ltd   ISBN 978-981-4629-63-8

Excerpt from *The Peculiar Pumpkin Thief*
(Originally published in Italy by Edizioni Piemme *Lo strano caso della Torre Pagliaccia*)

 **Circle the correct answers.**

1. What was **TRICKS FOR TAILS**?

    (a)   It was a party store selling decorations, weird gadgets and party pranks.

    (b)   It was a store selling giant pumpkins.

    (c)   It was a store selling spooky items.

    (d)   It was a store for customers to test their pranks.

2. ""Got ya!" **Paws** guffawed." What do you think "guffawed" means?

    (a)   Shouted

    (b)   Whispered

    (c)   Giggled softly

    (d)   Laughed loudly

3. Why would **Paws Prankster** test his pranks on his customers?

    (a)   To make them laugh

    (b)   To see if they work

    (c)   To scare them away

    (d)   He gets bored easily.

4. Why was there a *banana peel* on top of the pumpkin?

    (a)   It was part of the costume.

    (b)   It belonged to Paws who forgot to throw it away.

    (c)   It made the costume look more spooky.

    (d)   It belonged to Hercule Poirat who was hiding in the pumpkin costume.

5. Why couldn't they decide on a costume?

    (a)   The costumes were too scary.

    (b)   The costumes were not nice.

    (c)   They liked all the costumes.

    (d)   They had many days to decide.

 Excerpt from *The Peculiar Pumpkin Thief*
(Originally published in Italy by Edizioni Piemme *Lo strano caso della Torre Pagliaccia*)

© 2015 Scholastic Education International (S) Pte Ltd ISBN 978-981-4629-63-8

Yoo-Hoo!

At Tricks For Tails Geronimo and Benjamin discovered lots of decorations, gadgets and party pranks.

Match each item to the correct picture. Write the correct number.

1. Disgusting green slime
2. Plastic Swiss cheese with punching glove
3. Fluorescent fur dye
4. Giant bat with glow-in-the-dark eyes
5. Ghost costume
6. Bogeyman
7. Rubber snake
8. Jack-o'-lantern
9. Stink bombs
10. Hairy spiders
11. Plastic skull
12. Spider magnet
13. Squirt ring

Excerpt from *The Peculiar Pumpkin Thief* (Originally published in Italy by Edizioni Piemme *Lo strano caso della Torre Pagliaccia*)

Halloween is nearly here! There's so much to do.

The morning before Halloween, I woke up **early**. I had a lot to do to prepare for my Halloween party. I was sweeping my stoop when I noticed a bright orange-colored envelope in my mailbox. On it was written: **"Open . . . if you dare!"**

Inside was a sheet with a strange poem:

On the back of the invitation was a map on how to get to Mystery Park. It was all very **STRANGE**. I mean, I'd never even heard of a place called **Mystery Park**.

I decided to make some **hot cheddar**. Sometimes I think more clearly with a **steamy** mug of **hot cheddar** in my paws. I was still trying to make sense of the invitation when my doorbell rang.

X: Mystery Park

It was my cousin Trap, my sister, Thea, and my nephew Benjamin. Each of them was waving an **ORANGE** envelope.

Chew on it!

1. Does Geronimo dare?

Open...if you dare!

...to my Halloween party.

Please do your best not to be tardy.

I've planned a great night full of games and prizes.

And all the best music, rides, and surprises.

Candy corn, caramel apples, and, of course, lots of cheese.

The food is all free — eat as much as you please!

You don't know my name, but we'll meet tomorrow night:

Come to Mystery Park when the moon's shining bright.

Excerpt from *The Peculiar Pumpkin Thief*
(Originally published in Italy by Edizioni Piemme *Lo strano caso della Torre Pagliaccia*)

© 2015 Scholastic Education International (S) Pte Ltd   ISBN 978-981-4629-63-8

"Hey, Gerry Berry, I see you got the invite, too!" my cousin squeaked. "Fabarooni! We can all go **together**!"

I chewed my whiskers.

"Not so fast, Trap," I warned. "How do we even know who sent this? I don't like accepting invitations from STRANGERS."

Trap guffawed.

"Oh, don't get your fur in a frenzy, Geronimoid. Everybody's going. Plus, someone stole all the HALLOWEEN stuff in town. How else are you going to celebrate?" my cousin demanded.

Then he added, "And, you don't even need a costume, Cousinkins. You've already got a face like a Zombie."

I ignored him.

"Why don't you all come to **my house** instead?" I asked. "We don't need DECORATIONS to have fun on HALLOWEEN."

Trap smirked. Thea rolled her eyes. And Benjamin's shoulders SLUMPED. "Are you sure you don't want to go to the party, Uncle Geronimo?" he asked.

I gave in.

How could I say no to my favorite nephew?

2. Do Trap, Thea and Benjamin think a party at Geronimo's house will be fun?

Excerpt from *The Peculiar Pumpkin Thief*
(Originally published in Italy by Edizioni Piemme *Lo strano caso della Torre Pagliaccia*)

Circle the correct answers.

1. Geronimo made himself a mug of **hot cheddar**...

    (a) because his paws were cold.

    (b) as he was hungry.

    (c) to help him think.

    (d) because it is what he drinks when it's Halloween.

2. Why didn't Geronimo want to go to the party?

    (a) He thought it might be dangerous.

    (b) His party would be a lot better than the mystery one.

    (c) He had already prepared everything for his party.

    (d) He wouldn't know anyone at the party.

3. What did Trap mean when he said "Fabarooni!"?

    (a) Fabulous!

    (b) It is the name of Trap's car.

    (c) Trap was hungry and he was thinking of macaroni and cheese.

    (d) Oh no!

4. Why did Trap guffaw?

    (a) He felt that Geronimo was worrying way too much.

    (b) The mystery park was going to be fun.

    (c) Geronimo chewing his whiskers was funny.

    (d) Geronimo has a face like a zombie.

5. Why did Geronimo give in and agree to go to the party?

    (a) He wanted to prove to Trap that he was not afraid.

    (b) He did not want to disappoint Benjamin.

    (c) He did not want to make Thea angry.

    (d) He could save money by not having the party at his house.

 Excerpt from *The Peculiar Pumpkin Thief*
(Originally published in Italy by Edizioni Piemme *Lo strano caso della Torre Pagliaccia*)

© 2015 Scholastic Education International (S) Pte Ltd ISBN 978-981-4629-63-8

Do You 💀 Dare?

 Inside the mystery envelope was a sheet with a strange poem. Use the words to complete the invitation.

tardy	cheese	please	bright
surprises	prizes	party	night

You're invited to my
Halloween _____,

Please do your best
not to be _____.

I've planned a great night
full of games and _____,

And all the best music,
rides, and _____.

Candy corn, caramel apples, and,
of course, lots of _____,

The food is all free —
eat as much as you _____!

You don't know my name, but
we'll meet tomorrow _____:

Come to Mystery Park when the
moon's shining _____.

Excerpt from *The Peculiar Pumpkin Thief*
(Originally published in Italy by Edizioni Piemme *Lo strano caso della Torre Pagliaccia*)

Up in the air, we are on the run for our lives!

"We're being followed!" I shrieked in a panic as the clown copters grew closer.

But **Hercule** just laughed. That mouse loves a challenge. With a gleeful **squeak**, he yanked on the control stick, then began doing **somersaults** in midair.

A wave of nausea hit me. I grabbed an airsickness bag.

"Weak stomach, Geronimo?" Hercule smirked.

I couldn't answer. I was turning as **GREEN** as a stalk of celery.

Did I mention that I get airsick? And carsick. And seasick.

Oh, and I also get sick when I watch clothes *tumbling* around in the dryer at the Squeaky Clean Laundromat. But that's another story.

Even though my stomach was hurting, I still noticed the **STRANGE** activity going on in the streets far below. **Clowns** were everywhere. They were **rANsaCKiNG**

Chew on it!

1. What was the challenge?

Excerpt from *The Peculiar Pumpkin Thief*
(Originally published in Italy by Edizioni Piemme Lo strano caso della Torre Pagliaccia)

© 2015 Scholastic Education International (S) Pte Ltd ISBN 978-981-4629-63-8

the city! Houses, stores, banks. The clowns were stealing everything!

Luckily, **Hercule** was able to lose the clown helicopters that were chasing us.

"**Another job well done!**" hc congratulated himself. Then he pulled a bañaña out of his coat pocket.

"I **really** deserve a little snack," he announced as he SHOVED the fruit in his mouth and flipped the peel over his shoulder.

But the peel got **STUCK** under the control panel.

"**Oops**," Hercule muttered.

Two minutes later, the helicopter began sputtering in the air.

I looked out the window and saw the sea under us.

The **WAVES** were getting nearer and nearer and nearer!

SPLASHHH!

Before I could scream, we hit the water. The helicopter began to SINK.

glub glub glub glub glub glub glub...

2. Will Geronimo and Hercule escape the sinking helicopter?

Excerpt from *The Peculiar Pumpkin Thief*
(Originally published in Italy by Edizioni Piemme *Lo strano caso della Torre Pagliaccia*)

A Little Snack

Circle the correct answers.

1. Where were **Hercule** and Geronimo?

    (a) In a helicopter

    (b) In an airplane

    (c) At the laundromat

    (d) In a submarine

2. Why was Geronimo's stomach hurting?

    (a) He was airsick.

    (b) He was seasick.

    (c) He was turning into celery.

    (d) A wave hit him.

3. What was the **STRANGE** activity going on in the streets below?

    (a) Clowns were doing tricks.

    (b) Clowns were stealing and damaging everything.

    (c) Clowns were waving at Geronimo and Hercule.

    (d) Strange clowns were running about.

4. Why did Hercule eat a **banana**?

    (a) It was teatime.

    (b) He did not want his banana to get squashed in his coat.

    (c) Flying a helicopter makes him hungry.

    (d) He wanted to reward himself for escaping from the clown copters.

5. Why were the **WAVES** getting nearer and nearer?

    (a) Hercule was flying close to the sea where it was cooler.

    (b) They were trying to escape the clown copters.

    (c) The helicopter was going to crash.

    (d) They were taking a closer look at the strange things happening in the street.

 Excerpt from *The Peculiar Pumpkin Thief*
(Originally published in Italy by Edizioni Piemme *Lo strano caso della Torre Pagliaccia*)

 ISBN 978-981-4629-63-8

A Little  Snack

What was happening when these things were heard? Complete the table. The first one has been done for you.

	Who said it?/What made the sound?	What was happening?
We're being followed!	Geronimo	The clown copters were following Geronimo and Hercule.
Weak stomach, Geronimo?		
I really deserve a little snack		
Oops		
SPLASHHH!		
glub glub glub…		

Excerpt from *The Peculiar Pumpkin Thief* (Originally published in Italy by Edizioni Piemme *Lo strano caso della Torre Pagliaccia*)

MAKE A HALLOWEEN DECORATION

Match the step to the correct picture to make the decorations for an awesome party. Then label the final decorations *Scary Ghost* or *Bat Napkin Holder*.

1. Take a balloon, inflate it, and tie it with a long string.

2. In the center of a sheet of tissue paper large enough to cover the balloon, cut a small hole for the string. Be sure to use safety scissors!

5. Draw a bat on a piece of construction paper.

6. Cut along its edges, and then cut an opening along the mouth. Be sure to use safety scissors.

Excerpt from *The Peculiar Pumpkin Thief*
(Originally published in Italy by Edizioni Piemme *Lo strano caso della Torre Pagliaccia*)

© 2015 Scholastic Education International (S) Pte Ltd ISBN 978-981-4629-63-8

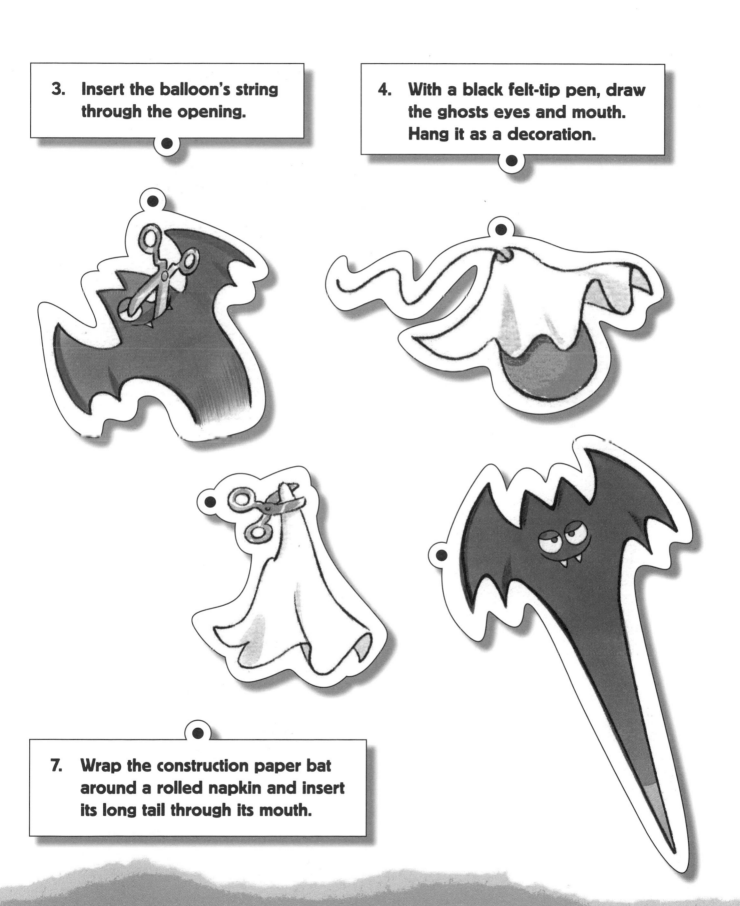

3. Insert the balloon's string through the opening.

4. With a black felt-tip pen, draw the ghosts eyes and mouth. Hang it as a decoration.

7. Wrap the construction paper bat around a rolled napkin and insert its long tail through its mouth.

Excerpt from *The Peculiar Pumpkin Thief*
(Originally published in Italy by Edizioni Piemme *Lo strano caso della Torre Pagliaccia*)

Answers

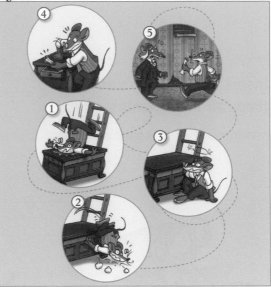

Section 1
Unit 1
Pages 6–7
Whilst-reading questions:
1. Uncle Stingysnout was sad that Geronimo was leaving.
2. i) Geronimo should leave because he has already helped his uncle in the garden. OR
   ii) Geronimo should stay and spend time with his dying uncle.
3. Geronimo was shocked because one small request had turned into seven requests.

Page 8
1. d   2. c   3. a   4. b   5. b

Page 9

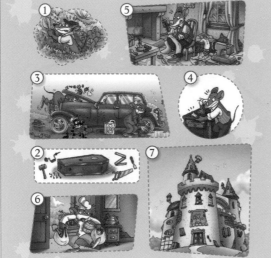

Unit 2
Pages 10–11
Whilst-reading questions:
1. A suspicious-looking smile is one that suggests a person cannot be trusted.
2. Accept all reasonable answers.
3. No, because when Geronimo passed Uncle Stingysnout the scroll, he quickly took it away, as if he was worried Geronimo would find out what he was hiding.

Page 12
1. b   2. a   3. c   4. c   5. b

Unit 3
Pages 14–15
Whilst-reading questions:
1. The castle is very big so there would be a lot of work to do.
2. i) No, because it is too much work for just one mouse. Geronimo may not know how to do everything. Uncle Stingysnout should not be so stingy and hire others to do it. OR
   ii) The list is fair because Uncle Stingysnout is too old to do it himself. Geronimo is young and strong.
3. Accept all reasonable answers.

Page 16
1. d   2. a   3. c   4. b   5. c

Page 17

Activity 1
Pages 18–19
1. so it does not get used up.
2. so he does not have to buy new tea bags.
3. so that he can save water by not bathing.
4. so that he could save his breath.

5. so that he would not have to buy wood.
6. so that he can save money on electricity.

Section 2
Unit 4
Pages 20–21
Whilst-reading questions:
1. shouted, yelled, hollered — Uncle Samuel was shouting at Geronimo and not speaking to him nicely.
2. Accept all reasonable answers.
3. Accept all reasonable answers.

Page 22
1. d   2. a   3. c   4. a   5. b

Page 23
Thea thinks it is <u>too cold</u> at the castle because Uncle Samuel won't <u>turn on the heat</u>.

Trap thinks that Uncle Samuel is too stingy to <u>put cheese</u> in the fridge so there is always <u>nothing to eat</u> there.

Benjamin finds the castle <u>dark</u> and <u>spooky</u> because Uncle Samuel won't spend the money to <u>turn on the lights</u>.

Unit 5
Pagess 24–25
Whilst-reading questions:
1. The Stiltons don't like the Stingysnouts because the latter are so cheap.
2. You save money on washing powder and water.
3. Accept all reasonable answers.

Page 26
1. b   2. a   3. a   4. b   5. d

Page 27
Method 1: read his newspaper
Method 2: without soap
Method 3: toilet paper ; underwear
Method 4: pants ; wash them
Method 5: my tea bags
Method 6: dental floss

Unit 6
Pages 28–29
Whilst-reading questions:
1. He had no candle and could not see well as he walked down the stairs.
2. Accept all reasonable answers.
3. They would not find anything in the coffin because Geronimo had said that it was unusually light.

Page 30
1. b   2. c   3. a   4. d   5. a

Page 31
1. windy; curtains
2. Lightning bolts; shadows
3. windows
4. dark; candles
5. leaking

Activity 2
Pages 32–33
Stevie: soaps
Chintzina: energy
Thriftella: free samples
Samuel S. Stingysnout: neighbor's newspapers
Penniford and Saveanna: taking one lick at a time
Worthington: three
Frugella: fat-free cheese
Michael Misermouse: ancient sculptures
Ivy: save her breath
Hoarden Accounts: heat
Zelda: steel
Grandma Cheaperly: recycles old bedsheets
Grandpa Cheaperly: shoes

Section 3
Unit 7
Pages 34–35
Whilst-reading questions:
1. warm and sunny, blue skies
2. Accept all reasonable answers.

Page 36
1. a   2. c   3. d   4. b   5. a

Page 37
1. cheese   2. sip   3. lucky
4. love   5. dark   6. pitch
7. darkness   8. wait

Accept all reasonable answers.

Unit 8
Pages 38–39
Whilst-reading questions:
1. Geronimo thought he would not get out of the elevator and would die there. His fur would remain in the elevator.
2. He wanted to get Geronimo's attention.
3. Bruce is probably going to take Geronimo somewhere and make him do something adventurous.

Page 40
1. c   2. a   3. c   4. d   5. d

Page 41
RULE NO. 1: RUN AWAY
RULE NO. 2: SCREAM
RULE NO. 3: CHEESE
RULE NO. 4: DANGEROUS
RULE NO. 5 and 6: Accept all reasonable answers.

Unit 9
Pages 42–43
Whilst-reading questions:
1. They were likely to go to a desert.
2. He knew that Geronimo was feeling uncomfortable.

Page 44
1. a   2. b   3. a   4. b   5. c

Page 45
The Sahara is the largest <u>desert</u> in the world. It is almost <u>four million</u> square miles. It is very <u>hot</u> there and can get up to <u>one hundred degrees</u> Fahrenheit even in the shade.

It is a place with lots and lots of <u>sand</u>. It is very <u>dry</u> because it never rains there.

There are a lot of <u>camels</u> that live in the desert and they are often used by the nomads for transportation.

Activity 3
Pages 46-47
Desert Survival Gear:
- Bandages for blisters
- Barrier skin cream
- Hiking boots
- Energy bars
- Glasses for the wind, fog, and sun
- Snake and scorpion anti-venom kit
- Mirrored sunglasses
- Sun hat
- Water bottle and drink mix
- Sunblock

North Pole Survival Kit:
- Breathable waterproof jacket
- Breathable waterproof pants
- Triple-layer wool sweater
- Snout mask with insulated lining
- Ear muffs
- Flashlight
- Heavy scarf
- Hiking boots
- Heavy wool socks
- Snowshoes
- Thermos
- Waterproof tail cover
- Lined gloves
- Thermal tent

Section 4
Unit 10
Pages 48–49
Whilst-reading questions:
1. He would test out his pranks on Geronimo.
2. A scary costume.
3. Accept all reasonable answers.

Page 50
1. a   2. d   3. b   4. d   5. c

Page 51

Unit 11
Pages 52–53
Whilst-reading questions:
1. Yes he does. He opens the envelope.
2. No, they do not.

Page 54
1. c   2. a   3. a   4. a   5. b

Page 55
party; tardy; prizes; surprises; cheese; please; night; bright

Unit 12
Pages 56–57
Whilst-reading questions:
1. The challenge was to escape from the clown copters.
2. Accept all reasonable answers.

Page 58
1. a   2. a   3. b   4. d   5. c

Page 59

	Who said it?/What made the sound?	What was happening?
We're being followed!	Geronimo	The clown copters were following Geronimo and Hercule.
Weak stomach, Geronimo?	Hercule	Geronimo was airsick after Hercule did somersaults in the helicopter.
I really deserve a little snack	Hercule	After Hercule escaped from the clown copters, he took out a banana to eat.
Oops	Hercule	Hercule threw the banana peel over his shoulder but it got stuck in the controls.
SPLASHHH!	Helicopter	The sound the helicopter made when it crashed into the sea.
glub glub glub…	Helicopter	The sound the helicopter made as it sunk.

Pages 60–61

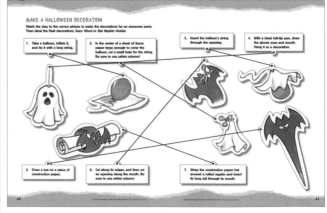

© 2015 Scholastic Education International (S) Pte Ltd   ISBN 978-981-4629-63-8